Alphabet

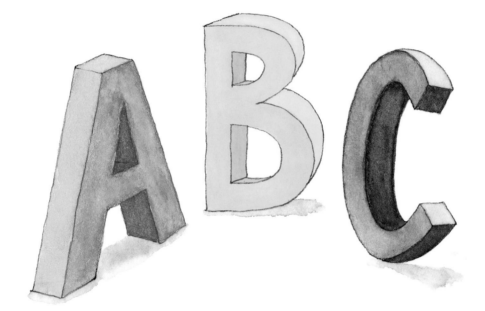

El alfabeto

el alfa*beh*-to

Catherine Bruzzone

Illustrations by Louise Comfort
Ilustraciones de Louise Comfort

b small publishing
www.bsmall.co.uk

Aa ambulance
la ambulancia

ah   lah amboo-*lan*-thee-a

This book belongs to

....

Este libro pertenece a

To parents and teachers

We hope this book will be fun to use in either English or Spanish. Here are a few helpful tips:

- When you start a foreign language, it's comforting and very useful to learn words which are similar to your own language, like the words in this book.

- Although the words and letters look very similar in Spanish and English, they are not usually *spoken* the same way. Have fun pronouncing the foreign language together. Use the pronunciation guide if necessary.

- Don't worry if your pronunciation isn't absolutely correct. The pronunciation guide will help but it cannot be completely accurate. You should read it as naturally as possible, but don't roll the r. Put stress on the letters in *italics* e.g. bal-*on*. Move on as soon as possible to speaking the words without the guide. Ask a Spanish-speaking person to help you if you can.

- There are three extra letters in the Spanish alphabet: ch, ll and ñ. These are included in the book with a sample word but no illustration.

- Encourage the children to have a go and give lots of praise. Little children are usually quite unselfconscious and this is excellent for building up confidence in a foreign language.

- Use the full alphabet at the top of the page to learn the alphabetical order. Try saying the whole alphabet in English and Spanish and answer the quiz questions at the end of the book.

- Finally, use the beautiful frieze as a talking point: the children can pick out objects they know in Spanish and perhaps learn new words too. They can also make up stories about the little characters and the exotic locations.

This edition first published 2008 by b small publishing ltd., The Book Shed, 36 Leyborne Park, Kew, Richmond, Surrey, TW9 3HA, UK
www.bsmall.co.uk
ISBN-13: 978-1-905710-49-2   All rights reserved.   © b small publishing ltd., 2008   5 4 3 2 1
Spanish Caterina Maluenda & Rosa Martín   *Editorial* Catherine Bruzzone & Susan Martineau
Design Lone Morton & Scott Gibson   *Production* Madeleine Ehm
Colour Reproduction Vimnice Printing Press Co. Ltd. *Printed in China* by WKT Company Ltd.

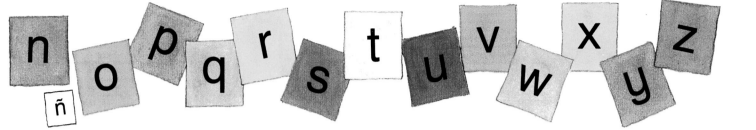

n ñ o p q r s t u v w x y z

Bb

ball
el balón

beh

el bal-*on*

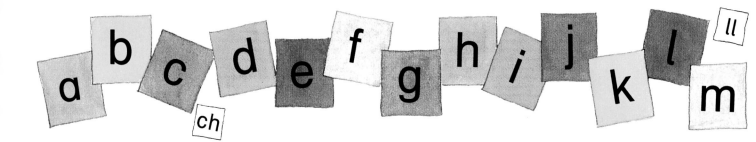

a b c d e f g h i j k l m
ch ll

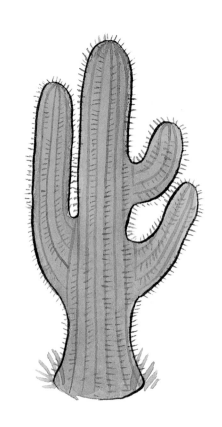

ch **chocolate**
cheh el chocolate
el choko-lah-teh

Cc **cactus**
el cactus

seh el *kak*-toos

Dd dolphin
el delfín

deh   el del-*fin*

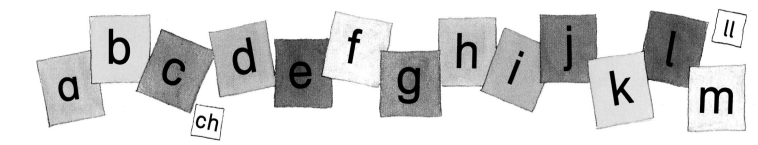

Ee elephant
el elefante

eh   el eleh-*fan*-teh

Ff fire
el fuego

effeh el foo-*ay*-go

Gg gorilla
el gorila

geh   el goh-*ree*-lah

n ñ o p q r s t u v w x y z

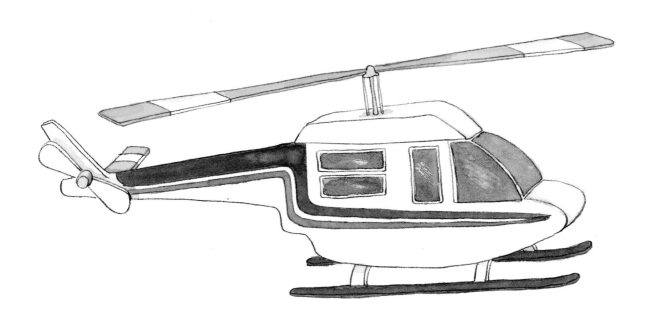

Hh helicopter
el helicóptero

*a*cheh

el elee-*kop*-tairo

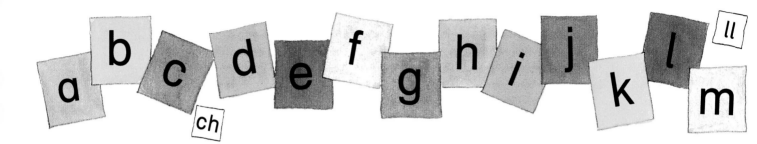

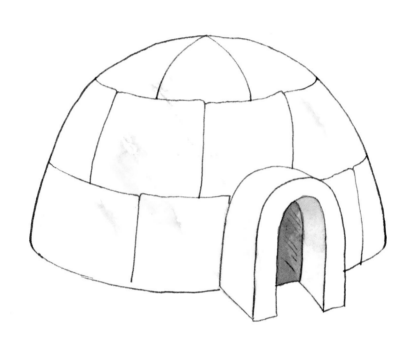

Ii igloo
el iglú

ee   el eeg-*loo*

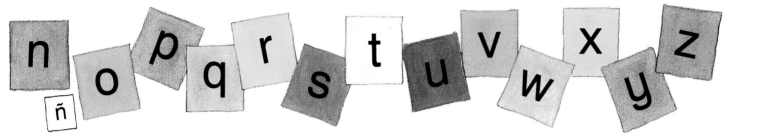

n ñ o p q r s t u v w x y z

Jj jungle
la jungla

*ho*ta   lah *hoon*-glah

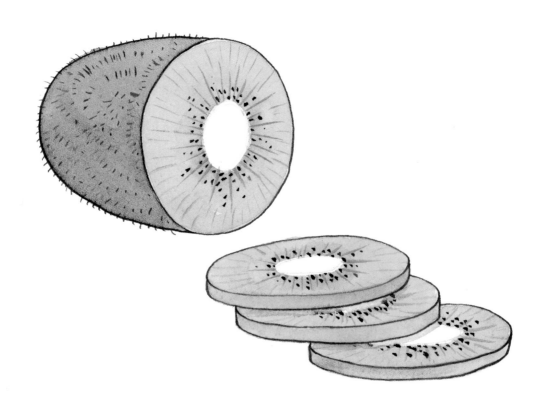

Kk kiwi
el kiwi

kah   el *kee*-wee

n ñ o o p q p r r s t u u v w x y y z

Ll **lion**
el león

*ele*h   el lay-*on*

ll **llama**
la llama
dobleh-eleh   lah *yah-mah*

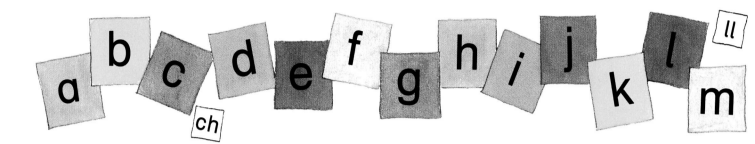

Mm mountain
la montaña

*em*eh   lah mon-*tan*-yah

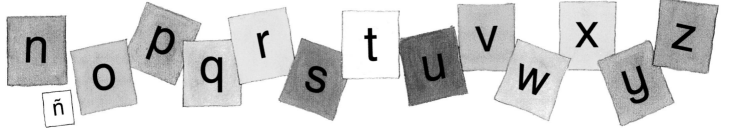

Nn

night
la noche

ñ **gnu**
el ñu

enyeh el n-yoo

*en*eh

lah *noh*-chay

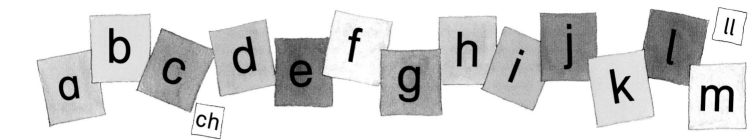

Oo **ogre**
el ogro

o'   el *o*-groh

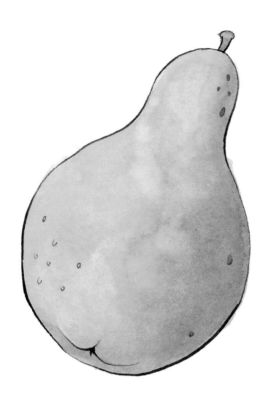

Pp pear
la pera

peh   lah *pair*-ah

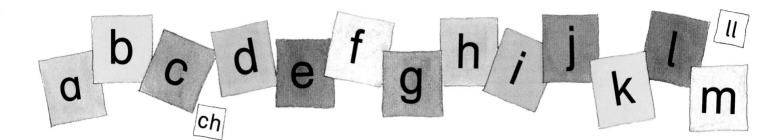

Qq

quintuplets
las quintizillas

koo

las kin-tee-*see*-yass

Rr reindeer
el reno

*air*eh el *ray*-noh

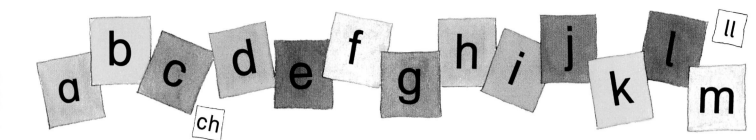

Ss sun
el sol

es-seh   el sol

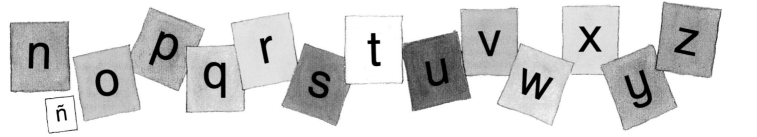

n ñ o p q r s t u v w x y z

Tt tomato
el tomate

teh　　　　　　el tom-*ah*-teh

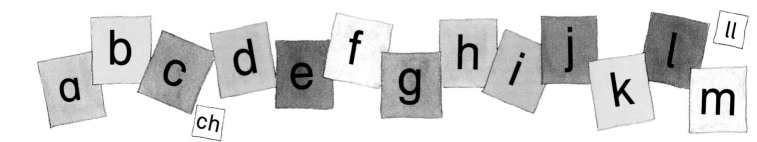

Uu

universe

el universo

oo

el oonee-*vair*-soh

Vv violin
el violín

veh   el veeyo-*leen*

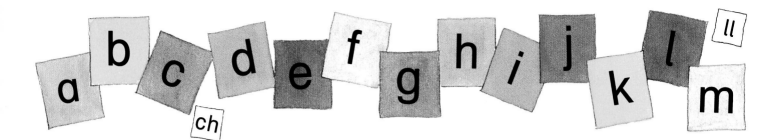

Ww **wok**
el wok

dob-leh veh/*oo*-veh   el wok

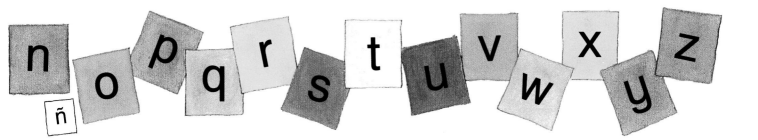

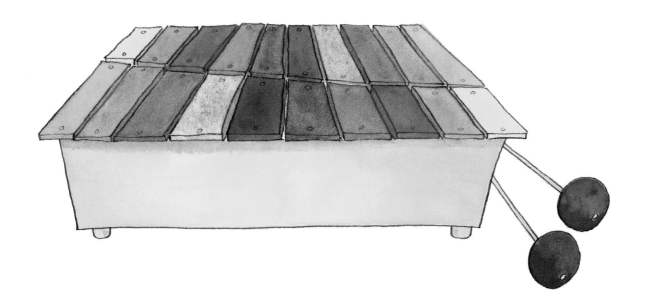

Xx xylophone
el xilófono

*ek*ees   el see-*lo*-fon-oh

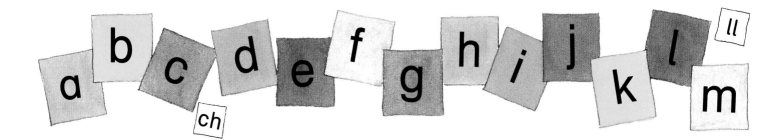

Yy yacht
el yate

ee gree-*eh*-gah   el *yat*-eh

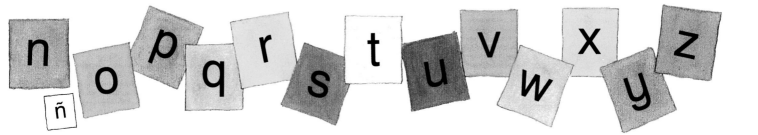

n ñ o o p q r r s t u u v w x y y z

Zz **zoo**
el zoo

*se*ta   el soh

The End

Fin

feen

ABC QUIZ

Read these aloud in Spanish, in the **correct** alphabetical order.

 el **b**alón

 el **h**elicóptero

 la **a**mbulancia

 el **i**glú

 el **c**actus

 el **g**orila

Can you say the names for the following pictures in Spanish?
Now say them in alphabetical order.

j

v

d

l

s

n

p

m

t

 b c d e g i k m

What are the missing letters?
Say them out loud in Spanish. Now say the whole alphabet.

 n o  s t u  w  y z

Check the answers by looking back through the book.

Other titles in this series:

ISBN: 978-1-905710-48-5

ISBN: 978-1-905710-47-8

b small publishing

If you have enjoyed this book, look out for our
other language learning books for children.
Order them from any good bookshop or request a catalogue from:
b small publishing ltd.
The Book Shed, 36 Leyborne Park, Kew, Surrey, TW9 3HA, UK
email: books@bsmall.co.uk
website: www.bsmall.co.uk